Where to Put the Ladder

Where to Put the Ladder

Experiencing the Power of God in Your Life

Dick Hochreiter
with
Erik V. Sahakian

WILDWOOD IGNITED

PUBLISHING

Cover Design/Layout/Photo: Andrew Enos
Editing/Formatting: Erik V. Sahakian

All Scripture is taken from the New King James Version of the
Bible. Copyright © 1979, 1980, 1982 by Thomas Nelson, Inc.
Used by permission. All rights reserved.

Library of Congress Control Number: 2017948828

ISBN 978-0-9852857-6-0
First Printing: November 2017

FOR INFORMATION CONTACT:

Wildwood Ignited Publishing:
A Ministry of Wildwood Calvary Chapel
35145 Oak Glen Rd
Yucaipa, CA 92399
www.wildwoodcalvary.com

Printed in the United States of America

CONTENTS

For my wife, Carol, who led me to Jesus so many years ago, and has stood by my side all the years since.

1

How I Lost My Job Over a Ladder

Many years ago, I was in a deacons meeting and was asked to share a short devotional. I shared from Luke 4:18, where Jesus says:

> The Spirit of the Lord is upon Me, because He has anointed Me to preach the gospel to the poor; He has sent Me to heal the brokenhearted, to proclaim liberty to the captives and recovery of sight to the blind, to set at liberty those who are oppressed.

I told them I believed this is what Jesus came to do and that He wants us to do the same today in His name. From the reaction I received I quickly realized not everyone was as enthusiastic about that calling as I was!

Later, during the same meeting, we were trying to make a decision about where to put a 40-foot ladder for a project. It seemed to go on forever and I remember thinking, *There are spiritually lost people in this city who don't know Jesus and we're trying to figure out where to put the ladder?*

Now, what I said next I would not say the same way today. I used to be an impatient man and over time I've become more gracious and merciful in how I speak to people, especially when we disagree. But back then, I was still young in my faith and I didn't hide my annoyance with others very well.

So raising my hand, I said, "I know where to put the ladder! Who cares?" I'm just being honest about what I said; I'm not proud of it, but I was seriously frustrated that they were missing the bigger picture!

Now, in all fairness, that group of deacons was entrusted to work out the administrative functions of the church, and that is necessary and important. We all have different spiritual gifts and they each serve a purpose in the body of Christ. The truth is we *do* need people to figure out practical answers to questions like where to store a 40-foot ladder! I was simply plugged into a ministry that was the wrong fit for me. I'm not interested in the placement of ladders—I just want to reach people for Jesus!

Not surprisingly, the next day I was asked to step down from the deacons. I know it's a sad story. I lost my first job as a deacon, but within a couple of weeks I was asked to help out at the County jail. I started out setting up chairs with a bunch of older businessmen who came from the desert faithfully each week to share the gospel of Jesus Christ with the prisoners. This is where I would work every Tuesday night for the next four years.

I remember one night when I first started helping. It was stormy so I got there early. I set up all the chairs and got everything ready for the meeting.

As soon as I was done the guard came in saying it was time to start the meeting.

I explained that the rest of the team had not arrived yet. They were the ones that had the music and the message.

The guard replied, "Don't you have a message? Can't you tell them how much God loves them?"

I said, "Yes I can! Bring them in!"

I shared my testimony of how the love of God changed my life and that God was no respecter of persons, meaning if He did it for me He would do it for them.

I asked them to stand if they wanted to receive Jesus.

All fifty of them stood up.

I thought they must have misunderstood, so I told them to sit down and I said, "Do you understand what I'm asking you to do? If you want to receive Jesus in your heart and into your life, and ask Him to forgive you for all your sins, then please stand up."

All fifty of them stood up again.

I was shocked. I said, "Let's pray out loud and receive Christ into our lives and ask Him to forgive us for all our sins."

That night changed my life.

We went on to see thousands of men come to Christ in the four years I worked there. What a blessing!

I really started to believe that God cared more for people than I ever could! What a blessing to start to understand the love and compassion Jesus has for the lost.

This was the beginning of my journey in understanding how to live *from* the finished work of the cross.

2

Hopeless, Lonely, and Without Direction

(We Must Be Born Again)

When I first met my wife and we started dating, she was so pretty and fun to be with, and within a few months we knew we loved and cared for each other and wanted to be married.

I remember her asking me if I was a Christian. In my mind I thought *everyone* in America was a Christian, but then she asked if I had a personal relationship with Jesus.

I said, "No, I don't think so," and she asked me if I would like to have one.

She explained to me how Christ died for our sins and if I would like to receive Him as my Lord and Savior, then I would experience that love and forgiveness in my life.

I had just returned from the Vietnam War. I had many burdens and sins. Depression was bearing down on me and I was feeling very lost.

She said Jesus wanted to be my friend and come into my life, forgive me of my sins, and help me every day.

Who wouldn't want that? Yes, I would like to receive Christ! So I prayed to receive Him into my life and forgive me for my sins.

Immediately, I felt the burden and depression lift from my heart and relief flooded into my life. That's when I was born again.

My life started to change from that day and continues to this day. Praise God! It's a loving relationship that keeps growing.

In the Gospel of John, chapter 3, Jesus said, "Most assuredly, I say to you, unless one is born again, he cannot see the kingdom of God" (v. 3).

Later, in verse 16, Jesus tells us, "For God so loved the world that He gave His only begotten Son, that whoever believes in Him should not perish but have everlasting life."

I think sometimes people have the wrong idea about God. God did not send His Son into the world to condemn the world, but to save the world through Him.

Jesus came on a rescue mission—that's why He died on the cross.

John 1:12 says, "But as many as received Him, to them He gave the right to become children of God, to those who believe in His name."

If you haven't yet received Christ, now is a great time to pray and ask Him to come into your life to forgive you of all your sins.

Today, you could be forgiven and healed! Today, you could become a child of God who will one day see heaven. There is no better time to turn to Jesus than today!

3

Do You Feel Like a Coward When You Share the Gospel? Join the Club!

(We Must Be Filled with the Holy Spirit)

I remember when a friend of mine challenged me to start praying for the hardest to reach nations in the world.

At the time, my company was hundreds of thousands of dollars in debt, so I thought I could pray any prayer as boldly as I wanted since there was no way (I thought) that God would actually send me. Under the circumstances, it was easy to pray bold prayers—I had nothing to lose!

Then God told me to repent of my debt. The word "repent" actually means to change your mindset and therefore your behavior, so I repented and agreed with God. At the time, I did not yet understand how powerful it is to pray.

Within eighteen months of beginning to pray, we were totally out of debt and had enough money to go anywhere in the world to bring the gospel!

At the time, Mongolia was one of the hardest countries in the world to reach for Jesus. Through a friend who had been researching Mongolia, I was given the opportunity to go.

It was 1990 and the country was considered to be closed to the gospel of Jesus. In fact, Mongolia was a communist nation with only two known believers in the entire country and no history of the gospel ever being preached.

So the next thing I knew I was on a plane with a friend-of-a-friend from Ohio that I didn't even know. I had literally just met him at the airport!

We flew to Beijing, China, then took a train for two days across the Gobi Desert until we finally arrived in Ulaanbaatar, the capitol of Mongolia.

It was then, at the train station, that it seemed like every demon in hell was coming at us.

As we were met by our guide, who spoke very little English, I thought, *Now what, big shot? You're here. What do you think you're going to do?*

I had been a Marine in the war in Vietnam. I was scared plenty of times, but this level of fear was totally different.

I had never been in a spiritual battle like this where it felt like every demon in hell was telling us, "You're not going to get out of here. They will put you in jail if you open your mouth!"

I was trying to think of every Sunday school lesson I could remember and it all seemed so hopeless. My mind was racing. *Why am I not at home on the couch watching TV? This is a mistake! I should've listened to all the people that told me not to go!*

A couple of days into the trip I remember seeing a man in a wheelchair and I heard God say, "You should pray for him."

He will never be healed—it's just the devil trying to set me up.

I was walking away and again my mind was racing. *This is so hopeless. These must be the people that are going to be in hell. We just need to get on the train and go home!*

On the plane ride home I was telling God over and over how I had made a terrible mistake and would never go back there again. I got back to the United States feeling very defeated.

I was talking about what happened with a friend of mine who had been a missionary in Mexico and he said, "If you're going to go to these countries you're going to need more of God's power. Come to our Wednesday night Bible study."

Yeah, like another Bible study is going to help me!

So there I was sitting in the Bible study listening as the pastor taught about faith in the Word and at the end he looked at me and said, "Do I know you?"

I said, "No."

He continued, "God just gave me a word for you. He says next time He tells you to pray for the sick, do it!"

Right then and there I knew God had been with me all along in Mongolia and that I was going back because God truly loves people.

I also now understood that I would need all the loving power that God would give me through the Holy Spirit.

The pastor prayed for me that night and I was filled with the Holy Spirit.

I remember praying fervently with all my heart and soon my love and confidence started to grow in the Word of God.

On the next trip to Mongolia, we saw two people come to Jesus and be baptized.

Then, on the next trip, we were invited to the university to speak to the students and help them practice their English, while we shared the gospel, but no one responded. We seemed to hit a stone wall with only one more day left to share the gospel.

We knew that words alone weren't working. We needed God's power, not just words. So we prayed all night and the Lord showed us to pray for the sick.

The next day, while we were preaching, we saw a young lady who was sick, so we prayed for her and she was instantly healed. The other students who knew her were amazed and faith began to break out.

By the end of that week, we baptized the first 36 believers in that nation.

I hear today there are more than 40,000 believers!

What does this prove? We *need* the empowering of the Holy Spirit! No matter what you may think, you can only do so much in your own natural strength.

Remember that Peter was a coward at one point, but after the Holy Spirit came upon him at Pentecost, suddenly he is preaching boldly, fearlessly, and he's leading 3,000 people to a loving Jesus. We will all be cowards without the filling of the Holy Spirit.

Zechariah 4:6 states, "'Not by might nor by power, but by My Spirit,' says the Lord of hosts."

That is an important distinction that God is making. It's not our abilities that God is most interested in—it's our willingness to walk in the power of His Spirit!

That's what the power of God does! It will rock your world to its very foundation. In fact, in the New Testament, the Greek word for "power" when we speak of the Holy Spirit is the word *dunamis*, from which we get the words "dynamite" or "dynamic." So when speaking of the power of the Holy Spirit, we're speaking of an explosive, life-changing power!

Now, before we go any further, we should take a moment to truly understand what it means to be filled with the power of the Holy Spirit (also called the Baptism of the Holy Spirit). Let's consider a few important questions that need to be answered from God's Word.

What is the Baptism of the Holy Spirit?

To answer our first question, let's examine a statement that Jesus made to His disciples in John 14:16-17:

> And I will pray the Father, and He will give
> you another Helper, that He may abide with
> you forever—the Spirit of truth, whom the
> world cannot receive, because it neither sees
> Him nor knows Him; but you know Him, for
> He dwells *with* you and will be *in* you
> [emphasis added].

Let's begin by considering the words "with" and "in." When Jesus said the Holy Spirit dwelled with them, He used the Greek word *para* which means to be by their side. In other words, Jesus said to His disciples that the Holy Spirit was presently alongside them. But then He said in that same verse that the Holy Spirit would be in them. The Greek word for "in" is *en* and it means to be inside something.

Jesus was telling His disciples that at that exact moment the Holy Spirit was beside them (*para*), but soon He would be in them (*en*). Notice Jesus uses the phrase "will be in you." He's speaking of the future. So at that point the Holy Spirit was with them, but not yet in them.

So when did the Holy Spirit go from being by their side to actually dwelling in them? I believe we see this after the crucifixion and resurrection when we read in John 20:21-22:

> So Jesus said to them again, 'Peace to you! As the Father has sent Me, I also send you.' And when He had said this, He breathed on them, and said to them, 'Receive the Holy Spirit.'

Here the disciples received the Holy Spirit into themselves, but they still lacked that *dunamis* power they would need to change the world. How do we know they were still lacking something? Consider Jesus' statement to them in Acts 1:4-5:

> And being assembled together with them, He commanded them not to depart from Jerusalem, but to wait for the Promise of the Father, 'which,' He said, 'you have heard from Me; for John truly baptized with water, but you shall be baptized with the Holy Spirit not many days from now.'

Notice, Jesus said "shall be baptized." Again, Jesus was speaking of another event with the Holy Spirit which had not yet happened, even though they had already received the Holy Spirit in them back in John 20.

And what was that future event they were to wait for? It was the Baptism of the Holy Spirit. We see it just a few verses later in Acts 1:8 when Jesus tells them, "But you shall receive power when the Holy Spirit has come upon you."

Again, Jesus says they "shall receive" so He is speaking of a future event. We also see the word "power", or *dunamis* there. But notice in this verse that Jesus said they would receive power when the Holy Spirit had come "upon" them. Here He uses the Greek word *epi*. The word *epi* carries the idea that something comes upon or overflows from an object.

Do you see the progression and escalation here between John 14:27 and Acts 1:8?

Jesus was telling His disciples, who had previously only had the Holy Spirit beside them (*para*), but who was now in them (*en*) as a result of the finished work of the cross and their resulting regeneration, that they would soon receive the power of the Holy Spirit and that power would overflow (*epi*) from their lives.

And of course we know that promise was fulfilled on the Day of Pentecost in Acts 2:4 when we are told, "And they were all filled with the Holy Spirit."

Here's one more example. In Acts 8:14-17, Philip has taken the gospel to Samaria and multitudes of people in the city believe in the name of Jesus and are saved:

> Now when the apostles who were at Jerusalem heard that Samaria had received the word of God, they sent Peter and John to them, who, when they had come down, prayed for them that they might receive the Holy Spirit. For as yet He had fallen upon [*epi*] none of them. They had only been baptized in the name of the Lord Jesus. Then they laid hands on them, and they received the Holy Spirit.

In these verses you see another example of people who had accepted Christ as their Savior, but had not yet experienced the Baptism of the Holy Spirit. They already had the Holy Spirit, but they hadn't yet received the *dunamis* power that Jesus promised in Acts 1:8.

So here we have the answer to our first question. What is the Baptism of the Holy Spirit? It is an experience where the power of the Holy Spirit is poured upon and overflows from a believer, which is distinct from the Holy Spirit dwelling in a believer as a result of their regeneration.

This leads us to our second question that we need to answer.

Why Do We Need the Baptism of the Holy Spirit?

Look again at Acts 1:8 when Jesus tells His disciples:

> But you shall receive power when the Holy Spirit has come upon you [*epi*]; and you shall be witnesses to me in Jerusalem, and in all Judea and Samaria, and to the end of the earth.

Notice that Jesus was calling His disciples to be His witnesses to the entire world, but what had to happen first? The power of the Holy Spirit had to first "come upon" them. In other words, they had to first receive the Baptism of the Holy Spirit *before* they could be effective witnesses.

We see further evidence in the events documented in the book of Acts. For example, we are told in Acts 2:4, "And they were all filled with the Holy Spirit and began to speak with other tongues, as the Spirit gave them utterance."

By the end of that day 3,000 people were saved! But what came first? They were filled with the Holy Spirit.

We see another example in Acts 4:31 when we are told:

And when they had prayed, the place where they were assembled together was shaken; and they were all filled with the Holy Spirit, and they spoke the word of God with boldness.

Here we see that boldness to speak the Word of God was preceded by, once again, being filled with the Holy Spirit. Do you see the pattern?

Now we have the answer to our second question. Why do we need the Baptism of the Holy Spirit? We need it to be fully equipped to be used by God and to walk victoriously in the Christian life.

Hopefully at this point we realize two very important truths:

- A person can be saved, and have the Holy Spirit in them, yet not have received the Baptism of the Holy Spirit, that overflow of supernatural power.
- To be effective in Christian ministry and life, we desperately need the power that the Baptism of the Holy Spirit brings.

So if we may not have it, and we know that we need it, how do we get it? Let's finish up with our third and final question.

How Do We Receive the Baptism of the Holy Spirit?

In Acts 8, word gets back to Jerusalem about an amazing harvest of souls in Samaria, so Peter and John are sent to check it out. When they arrive they realize that the new Samaritan converts had believed in Jesus, which also meant the Holy Spirit was in them, but they had not experienced the power of the Holy Spirit coming upon them, so "they laid hands on them, and they received the Holy Spirit" (Acts 8:17).

We see after the laying on of hands, the people received the Baptism of the Holy Spirit. However, in the Bible the laying on of hands is not the only action that may precede the Baptism of the Holy Spirit.

Consider Acts 10, in the house of Cornelius:

> While Peter was still speaking these words, the Holy Spirit fell upon all those who heard the word. And those of the circumcision who believed were astonished, as many as came with Peter, because the gift of the Holy Spirit had been poured out on the Gentiles also (Acts 10:44-45).

So in Acts 10 we have an example of the Baptism of the Holy Spirit taking place *without* the laying on of hands. Peter was actually in the middle of a sermon when it happened! There are numerous other examples of the Baptism of the Holy Spirit following various activities throughout Acts, such as:

- Being in one accord together (Acts 2:1-4)
- Prayer (Acts 4:31)
- Laying on of hands (Acts 8:17; 9:17; 19:6)
- Preaching the Word (Acts 10:44)

Notice that though there are various activities that preceded the Baptism of the Holy Spirit, there is one factor that was common to all. Clearly, every individual who received the Baptism of the Holy Spirit was open, willing, and desired to receive it. In scripture, no one who received the Baptism of the Holy Spirit rejected or denied the opportunity. They all wanted it, and they all got it.

Now we come to the answer to our final question. How do we receive the Baptism of the Holy Spirit? With a willing and open heart, we ask God to baptize us with His Holy Spirit…again and again and again.

Remember back in the house of Cornelius, in Acts 10:45, the Baptism of the Holy Spirit is referred to as the "gift of the Holy Spirit"? The two terms are referencing the same *epi* experience—the overflow of *dunamis* power.

Well, remember Jesus said in Matthew 7:11, "how much more will your Father who is in heaven give good things to those who ask Him!"

If the Baptism of the Holy Spirit is a "gift" from God to us, and He wants us to ask for His gifts, then all we need to do is ask Him for *dunamis* power to live a victorious Christian life and to impact this world for His kingdom. We can pray that prayer with boldness and confidence knowing that it's already God's heart to answer that prayer.

A Heavenly Prayer Language

One of the byproducts of being filled with the Holy Spirit is that His power can be manifested in our lives through the gifts of the Holy Spirit. Now, we can devote an entire study to the gifts of the Holy Spirt, but for our purposes I would like to focus on just one—the gift of tongues.

People have made much controversy regarding this gift, which is unfortunate because it is such an important one. Due to incorrect teaching about what the Bible says about tongues, a lot of Christians are afraid of this gift—but they shouldn't be. I believe that fear is a specific strategy of our enemy to prevent us from desiring and using the gift of tongues.

Before I go any further, I want to preface the remainder of this chapter by pointing out that the Bible teaches on both the public use of tongues and the private use of tongues. Nearly all the controversy with tongues stems from its public use. There's a lot to be said about the public use of tongues, but what I want to focus on instead is its private use.

Some may consider it splitting hairs to differentiate between what we collectively define as the gift of tongues and what the Bible also refers to as praying in the spirit, but I see evidence of both.

Speaking in tongues is a gift for the body of Christ when combined with interpretation, but your heavenly prayer language is given to you to build up your own faith. Paul tells us in First Corinthians 14:4, "He who speaks in a tongue edifies himself." The word for "edifies" in Greek is *oikodomeo* which is a construction term that literally means to build something. Perhaps not many of us will ever stand in front of a congregation and speak in tongues, but I'm confident that every one of us needs our personal faith to be built up and strengthened. It's a powerful gift.

One time in Cuba I was in a congregation where everyone was speaking Spanish. I was wondering if I spoke in tongues would there be any translation? No one translated, so I thought I must not have the gift of tongues. I could have translated it, then the interpreter would've translated it, but I thought maybe that would be cheating! Who knows?

All kidding aside, I do believe God wants believers to pray in the spirit to build themselves up. Does the Bible teach this? Absolutely! In Jude 20-21 we read:

> But you, beloved, building yourselves up on your most holy faith, praying in the Holy Spirit, keeping yourselves in the love of God, looking for the mercy of our Lord Jesus Christ unto eternal life.

The phrase "building up" is rooted in the same Greek word that's translated as "edify" in First Corinthians 14:4. So God wants us to be building ourselves up in faith. Did you catch the next part? Jude then references "praying in the Holy Spirit."

This is very similar to what Paul wrote in First Corinthians 14:15 when he states:

> What is the conclusion then? I will pray with the spirit, and I will also pray with the understanding. I will sing with the spirit, and I will also sing with the understanding.

Remember, the context of First Corinthians 14 is laying down the ground rules for exercising the gift of tongues. In verse 15, Paul is contrasting praying in the spirit versus praying with understanding. It is clear that to "pray with the spirit" therefore is just another way of saying praying in tongues.

God desires for our faith to be built up (edified). Every believer needs to be edified and the Bible teaches the gift of tongues edifies the believer. We may not all be called to publically exercise tongues in church, but every one of us could sure use tongues in our private prayer time. Perhaps that is why Paul said, "I wish you all spoke with tongues" (1 Corinthians 14:5).

I remember when I fell in love with my wife, Carol. I wanted to be with her all the time. I wanted to know everything about her—even to know her family and friends. I remember the excitement of being in love. There wasn't anything I wouldn't do for her.

I think this is the kind of passion Christ has for us and we need to have the same kind of loving relationship with Him. We need to open our hearts and be willing to receive whatever He has for us. Being filled with the Holy Spirit is probably one of the most loving gifts we could ever receive.

Think about this: The God of the universe who saved your soul wants you to have the loving power of His Holy Spirit in your life. We need to contend for it; we need to pursue it. We are told in First Corinthians 14:1-

2, "Pursue love, and desire spiritual gifts...For he who speaks in a tongue does not speak to men but to God." Our flesh and our minds don't want us to have this gift, but God does. Who will you obey?

Have you ever come to a place in prayer where you just don't have the words or it seems like you're hitting a wall? That is when I start praying in my heavenly prayer language.

So many times when I need help and I pray in the spirit, in my heavenly prayer language, God gives me the answers and revelations that I need to be able to do what is right and what He's asking me to do. The Holy Spirit is a powerful Helper and Comforter.

Just take time to pray and sit in God's presence and let Him speak to you. He truly loves you and will give you gifts if you ask, and as He determines. Will you ask? It's time to take a leap of faith in God.

Asking for the Gifts

Know this: God wants you to have His gifts more than you want them! Take God at His word and act on it. He has provided a way to receive the filling of the Holy Spirit. Don't be halfhearted; be wholehearted! Let's get over ourselves and put God first.

My hope is the following prayer will help encourage you in asking to be filled with the power of the Holy Spirit and also to receive your own heavenly prayer language:

Heavenly Father, I am a believer. I am Your child and You are my Father, my God. I believe with all my heart that Your Word is true. Please fill me and baptize me afresh in Your Holy Spirit. In the name of Jesus Christ, my Lord, I am asking You to fill me to overflowing with Your power. Jesus, fill me with the Holy Spirit that I may walk victoriously and that I might impact this world for You. Because of Your Word, I believe that I have now received Your gift and I thank You for it. I believe the Holy Spirit has filled me and, by faith, I accept Him. Now, Holy Spirit, please rise up within me as I praise God. I fully hope to speak with a heavenly prayer language, as You give me utterance. In Jesus' name. Amen (scripture references: Luke 11:10-13; 1 Corinthians 14:4; Jude 20; Acts 2:4).

Now begin to praise God for filling you with the Holy Spirit. Speak the words and syllables you receive—not in your own language, but the language given to you by the Holy Spirit.

You have to use your own voice. God will not force you to speak. Don't be concerned with how it sounds. The devil will tell you that's not it. Tell him from me to shut up! It is a heavenly language and it will grow and fill you with encouragement like never before.

Remember, don't lean on your own understanding (Proverbs 3:5-6). Acknowledge God. Don't let the devil talk you out of it. You need to practice and to fight for it. Don't just get it and stop using it. It's a powerful tool for prayer warfare. That's why every demon in hell doesn't want you to use it.

It's so simple even your computer can pray in the spirit! Remember, God chose the foolish things to confound the wise (1 Corinthians 1:26-29). Don't let this freak you out. Instead, go for it!

Now, a quick word of encouragement for those who prayed for a heavenly prayer language, but did not receive it—don't stop asking! God imparts His gifts of the Spirit as He wills and in His perfect timing (not ours). They are all gifts of grace. So keep desiring and asking for your heavenly prayer language, don't give up, and wait to see what God has planned.

Thank you, Jesus, for filling us today with Your Holy Spirit and for all Your gifts!

4

Can You Really Trust God's Word?

(We Must Be Believing Believers)

When my business was going broke and I had nowhere to turn but to God, all I had was His Word that if I seek first the kingdom of God and His righteousness, then all these things will be added to me (Matthew 6:33).

As I started seeking His kingdom, His word proved true. Then He gave me Romans 8:28—that He would work all things together for good, for those who love Him and are called according to His purpose—and He did!

Through praying in the spirit God will make His words come alive in our lives—you will believe and trust like never before. This is what we need to come *from* the finished work of the cross. We have to believe *everything* Christ did for us and act on it.

> For all the promises of God in Him are Yes, and in Him Amen, to the glory of

God through us. Now He who establishes us with you in Christ and has anointed us is God, who also has sealed us and given us the Spirit in our hearts as a guarantee (2 Corinthians 1:20-22).

And do not be conformed to this world, but be transformed by the renewing of your mind, that you may prove what is that good and acceptable and perfect will of God (Romans 12:2).

5

Ready to Live Out Loving Works

Now, it's time to go back to the ladder. Where do you think we should put the ladder? I decided to put the bottom of the ladder in my heart which is filled with the Holy Spirit, and the top of the ladder in heaven where Jesus sits at the right hand of the Father. By abiding in Him, I pray to always hear what God is saying to me and to be obedient to His call on my life.

Remember what Jesus said:

> Most assuredly, I say to you, he who believes in Me, the works that I do he will do also; and greater works than these he will do, because I go to My Father. And whatever you ask in My name, that I will do, that the Father may be glorified in the Son. If you ask anything in My name, I will do it (John 14:12-14).

By the way, I made seven more trips into Mongolia and helped to bring the kingdom of God to over thirty other countries, all from just that one night I went to a Bible study and was filled with the Holy Spirit.

Looking back at what the Lord did through my friends and me, at the time, seemed foolish, but 27 years later it's still the best move I've ever made for my life and the **kingdom of God.**

It reminds me of what was said in Acts 4:13-14:

> Now when they saw the boldness of Peter and John, and perceived that they were uneducated and untrained men, they marveled. And they realized that they had been with Jesus.

My prayer for you is that you will receive the Baptism of the Holy Spirit and that your heavenly prayer language will help you become a powerful prayer warrior for the kingdom. May you become a believing believer with all the power from heaven to fully believe and apprehend all that Christ did for us on the cross. In Jesus' name.

God bless…

Brother Dick

About the Authors

Dick Hochreiter was the president and owner of the Sportsgear Corporation in the USA, which produced private labeling of off-road clothing for large sporting goods companies. Through the challenges of running a corporation for 26 years, he saw firsthand how God could bring hope to the marketplace for business owners.

He has traveled to more than thirty countries, bringing the gospel into very desperate situations.

For the last seventeen years, he has run an anointing oil company called The Prayer Company, whereby he ships oils internationally. Please visit theprayercompany.com for more information.

In 2012, he and a friend started Jesus Food, packaging food for the starving all around the world. God has given him a vision for the eradication of starvation in all of Africa.

To learn more about this vision for Africa, please visit jesusfood.org and click on the Vision 2020 tab.

Erik V. Sahakian has committed his life to serving Jesus Christ through teaching God's inerrant Word, ministering to the body of Christ, and writing. He joyfully worships and serves with his wife and children at Wildwood Calvary Chapel in Yucaipa, CA. Visit eriksahakian.com to learn more.

www.ingramcontent.com/pod-product-compliance
Lightning Source LLC
Chambersburg PA
CBHW060544030426
42337CB00021B/4429